Life as a Ninja

An Interactive History Adventure

by Matt Doeden

Consultant:
Don Roley
Ninjutsu Research Specialist
Colorado Springs, Colorado

CAPSTONE PRESS
a capstone imprint

You Choose Books are published by Capstone Press,
1710 Roe Crest Drive, North Mankato, Minnesota 56003.
www.capstonepub.com

Library of Congress Cataloging-in-Publication Data
Doeden, Matt.
    Life as a ninja: an interactive history adventure / by Matt Doeden.
    p. cm. — (You choose — warriors)
    Includes bibliographical references and index.
    Summary: "Describes the lives of ninjas in feudal Japan. The reader's choices reveal historical
details from the perspectives of a ninja taking part in the siege of Sawayama Castle, fighting the
army of Oda Nobunaga, and serving as a member of the Band of Iga" — Provided by publisher.
    ISBN 978-1-4296-4027-5 (lib. bdg.)
    ISBN 978-1-4296-4867-7 (paperback)
    1. Ninja — Juvenile literature. 2. Ninjutsu — Juvenile literature. I. Title. II. Series.
UB271.J3D64 2010
355.5'48 — dc22   2009032951

Editorial Credits
Angie Kaelberer, editor; Veronica Bianchini, designer; Wanda Winch, media researcher;
    Laura Manthe, production specialist

Photo Credits
Alamy: Aflo Foto Agency/Fukuma Hidenori, 79; The Art Archive: Suntory Museum of Art
Tokyo/Laurie Platt Winfrey, 65, Tokyo National Museum/Granger Collection, 74, Tokyo
University/Laurie Platt Winfrey, 81, US Naval Academy Museum, 102; The Bridgeman
Art Library/(c)Look and Learn/Private Collection: 6, 40, Private Collection, 42; Capstone
Studio: Karon Dubke, cover (ninja); Getty Images Inc.: DEA Picture Library, 38; IGA-RYU
Ninja Museum, 85; Illustration from REAL NINJA, by James Field and Stephen Turnbull
and reproduced by permission of Breslich & Foss Ltd, London, (c) 2008: 24, 33, 61, 88;
iStockphoto: jecka, 16, Slavoljub Pantelic, 28; Osprey Publishing/Wayne Reynolds: 10, 12,
21, 34; Peter Newark's Pictures: 45, 70, 94, 100; Shutterstock: Emir Simsek, 55, Jaroslaw
Grudzinski, cover background, Jef Thompson, 104

Printed in the United States of America in Stevens Point, Wisconsin.
112012   007057R

TABLE OF CONTENTS

ABOUT YOUR ADVENTURE

YOU are living in Japan during a time known as the *Sengoku Jidai*, or Age of the Warring States. You are a ninja — a secret, deadly warrior. What kind of missions will you take on? What sort of decisions will you face?

In this book, you'll explore how the choices people made meant the difference between life and death. The events you'll experience happened to real people.

Chapter One sets the scene. Then you choose which path to read. Follow the directions at the bottom of each page. The choices you make will change your outcome. After you finish one path, go back and read the others for new perspectives and more adventures.

YOU CHOOSE the path
you take through history.

Samurai warriors fought in the open, unlike the skilled, secretive ninja.

Shadow Warriors

It was a time of violence and instability in Japan. From 1467 until about 1600, Japan was in a nearly constant state of war. The country was split into hundreds of small states. Each was led by a lord, or daimyo. These states fought for power. People called this time the Age of the Warring States.

Powerful samurai warriors served their masters, valuing honor above all else. Armies marched against one another. In the shadows lurked the ninja, or *shinobi*. These highly trained, secretive warriors were filled with mystery. Many were hired mercenaries. They sold their skills in the martial art of *ninjutsu* to the highest bidder.

7

Turn the page.

The first recorded acts of what we commonly think of as ninja date to the 1400s. But it's likely that the art of ninjutsu had been forming for hundreds of years before that. Stories of ninjalike activities stretch back at least to the 900s.

Ninjutsu began on the island of Honshu, the largest of Japan's four main islands. It was especially common in the province of Iga and county of Koga, where the most skilled ninja trained. Ninjutsu had roots in Japanese martial arts and military training. In the 900s, Chinese refugees who settled in Japan brought their skills in body conditioning and stealth to the art.

The ninja tradition was passed from parent to child and from teacher to student. Unlike the samurai warriors, social class did not matter. Anyone with skill and a willingness to work hard could become a ninja.

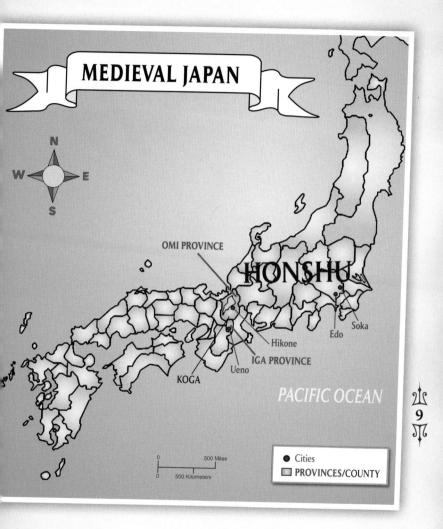

MEDIEVAL JAPAN

N
W E
S

OMI PROVINCE

HONSHU

Hikone

IGA PROVINCE

Ueno

KOGA

Edo

Soka

PACIFIC OCEAN

0   500 Miles
0   500 Kilometers

● Cities
☐ PROVINCES/COUNTY

Turn the page.

Young ninja practiced using weapons.

Most ninja were men, but women could train as well. Children began training at a very early age. They may have trained for 10 years or more. Young ninja learned fighting techniques and how to use weapons such as swords and throwing stars called *shuriken*. They learned survival skills, spy and observation methods, and how to disguise themselves.

As adults, ninja could take on many roles. They were warriors and bodyguards. They also were assassins, killing people their employers wanted dead. They disguised themselves and worked as spies. Above all else, they were skilled at blending in with the crowd. Whether a ninja was walking down the street or sneaking up a castle wall, the goal was to remain unnoticed.

Which secret mission will you accept?

➤ To help in the attack on an enemy castle in 1558, turn to page **13**.

➤ To defend your homeland from an enemy attack in 1581, turn to page **41**.

➤ To serve as a bodyguard to a powerful daimyo in 1600, turn to page **71**.

Ninja used a variety of weapons and equipment to help them carry out their missions.

CHAPTER 2

Siege of Sawayama Castle

You stand alone, looking up at the walls of Sawayama Castle near the city of Hikone. Activity buzzes all around you. You're a mercenary ninja, fighting for whomever pays the most for your services.

Today you're part of an army fighting under the command of Rokkaku Yoshikata, the samurai leader of the Rokkaku clan. The Rokkaku clan is allied with the Dodo clan, which holds the castle. A member of that clan, Dodo Kuranosuke, has rebelled against the Rokkaku clan. Yoshikata's goal is to drive Kuranosuke out of the castle.

Turn the page.

Samurai warriors strut around, giving orders to the soldiers. A tall, well-muscled samurai walks past you. He barely looks at you. The samurai know the ninja are a necessary part of the army, but they are uncomfortable with your secretive ways. They think your methods are dishonorable. They tend to avoid you whenever possible.

You don't mind. The samurai are welcome to their honor. Their honorable ways haven't helped them get inside the castle walls. For that, they need you.

You are one of about 50 ninja Yoshikata hired to take part in the siege. Your leader, Tateoka Doshun, is already forming plans on how to get inside. Doshun is a clever man and a respected ninja. But as night approaches, you can't help feeling that the time to strike is now.

The sooner this siege is over, the sooner you can return home to the province of Iga. Your 8-year-old daughter, Aya, is training in ninjutsu. You're eager to help her.

You stare at the castle wall. You know you could get inside. Then you could spy on the enemy or set fires that would drive Kuranosuke from hiding. But Doshun is your leader. He will have a plan, and it might be best to find out what it is.

→ To try to get inside the castle walls alone, turn to page **16**.

→ To wait for Doshun's plan, turn to page **19**.

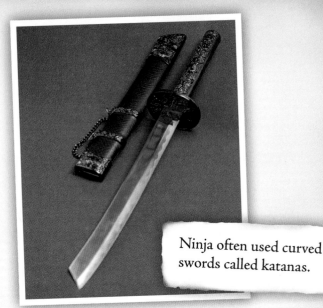

Ninja often used curved swords called katanas.

The sun has almost set. You're tired of waiting. It's time for action. You prepare yourself for your attack, telling no one. You dress in dark clothing so you'll be harder to see. A black hood called a cowl covers your head and face.

You look over your equipment carefully, deciding what to bring with you. First, you'll have to climb the castle wall. You grab a few tools for the job. Your *kaginawa* is a rope with a hook that will help you climb. You attach spikes called *tekkokagi* to your feet.

You wouldn't dare break into an enemy castle without weapons. Your *katana* is your best weapon. With its long, curved blade, the katana is a deadly sword, though not as large as a samurai's sword. You also bring several shuriken. You think about dipping the stars' tips into poison but decide there's no need. You're not on an assassination mission. Finally, you bring a tinderbox for setting fires. When you get inside, you'll want to create as much disorder as possible.

As you leave, someone calls out your name. "What are you doing?"

It is Tozawa, a fellow ninja. He is from a nearby village, and you've known him for years. You can trust him.

"I'm tired of waiting," you say. "It's time to take action."

Turn the page.

"It's a bad idea to go alone," Tozawa says with a smile. "I'm coming with you."

You sigh. You'd rather do this alone, but Tozawa is a skilled ninja. You decide to accept his help. "I'm planning to climb over the wall, collect some information, and set fires," you explain.

"We could dress as castle servants to get inside instead," Tozawa suggests. "It might be less dangerous."

→ To climb the wall, turn to page **21**.

→ To dress as servants to get inside, turn to page **23**.

As a ninja, you know that patience is one of your greatest weapons. You must wait for the perfect opportunity. You will see what Doshun has planned.

The next day, you find out. Doshun explains his simple but brilliant plan. He holds a paper lantern before his group of ninja. "We have stolen a lantern that carries the sign of the Dodo family name. The lantern was easy to copy. Tonight, these will be our passes through the front gate."

Beside you, a fellow ninja whispers, "*Bakemono-jutsu*." Doshun has proposed this "ghost technique," which is a classic ninja trick.

That night, the ninja gather. Several of them carry the fake Dodo lanterns, and you file through the front gate. The guards watch you with little interest.

Turn the page.

Just like that, you're inside! The enemy is doomed, and he doesn't even know it yet.

Doshun says softly, "Set fires and create a panic. Bring down our enemy." But you have a bigger idea in mind. If you could kill or capture Kuranosuke, Yoshikata would be especially grateful.

➛ To set fires, turn to page **25**.

➛ To search for Kuranosuke, turn to page **26**.

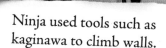

Ninja used tools such as kaginawa to climb walls.

It's pitch black as the two of you approach a section of the castle wall that appears unwatched. Wasting no time, you get to work. With a toss, you lodge the hook of your kaginawa onto the top of the wall and begin climbing. You stand atop the wall as Tozawa follows. You admire his skills. He moves like a shadow. If you didn't know he was there, you'd never see him.

Turn the page.

No one notices as the two of you climb down to an open courtyard. Together, you walk silently along the outside edge of the wall. You take note of the castle defenses, including half a dozen guards and some cannons. Ninja must always be fully aware of their surroundings. Your ability to gather information about your location and the enemy can be a matter of life and death.

"We should go," Tozawa whispers. "Let's tell Doshun what we've seen."

It might be a good idea. But you've come to do more than just gather information. You're inside the castle walls. It's a great chance to weaken the enemy. You've spotted an enemy storeroom. It's a perfect target for a fire.

➤ To leave now and bring the information back to Doshun, turn to page **31**.

➤ To set fire to the storeroom, turn to page **33**.

Tozawa is right. His idea would be less dangerous. You agree.

The two of you dress in the servants' clothes that you brought with you. You smile as you think about the trick. It is something no samurai would ever do. They are far too proud to even pretend to be a commoner.

You approach the main gate, with your eyes focused on the ground. You move your feet in a slow shuffle, trying to appear like you're not in any hurry. Tozawa follows just behind you.

"Stop!" a voice rings out. An enemy samurai is marching toward you. "Who are you?"

Your hand closes around the hilt of your katana, tucked underneath your clothing.

"Just humble servants," Tozawa says softly.

Turn the page.

Ninja sometimes disguised themselves as guards to enter castles.

The samurai draws a long sword. "I've never seen you before. You're coming with me!"

Tozawa shouts, "Run!" and darts back the way you came. The enemy samurai steps toward you, his sword raised.

→ To run, turn to page **37**.

→ To fight the samurai, turn to page **38**.

You have your orders. The ninja scatter around the castle to set their fires. You creep toward the castle's stables. There you kneel at one of the castle's wooden walls and carefully unwrap your tinderbox. You make a small pile of tinder and soak it in oil. With a strike of a small flint rock, the wall bursts into flames.

Calmly, you move back toward the gate. There's little time. Already, shouts are rising up around you as the guards discover the fires. Several of Kuranosuke's men rush right past you. They don't realize that you are an enemy. Doshun's plan has worked perfectly. As you watch the fires burn, you smile. Soon, you will return home to Iga and to your family. You can't wait to tell your daughter about your part in Doshun's plan.

Turn to page 36.

The other ninja scatter to set fire to the castle. Soon, the castle defenses will be overwhelmed.

You scan the castle grounds, looking for anyone of high rank. You move quickly, knowing that the fires will soon begin to spread. You pass several groups of soldiers, but no one important.

Suddenly, a cry arises in the castle. "Fire! We're under attack!"

The castle erupts in a panic. Shouts rise up from all around you. People are running in every direction. The castle defenders quickly realize that this must be only the first stage of an attack. And they're right. Yoshikata and his men will soon carry out a final attack.

For the moment, the castle's defenses are in a state of confusion. If you're to find Kuranosuke, the time is now.

Then you see him. In the distance, surrounded by guards, Kuranosuke rushes toward safety. You charge toward him, weaving through people and past guards. But before you can reach Kuranosuke, his guards notice you. Three of them fall back and stand in your way. One is a samurai.

"You will pay, ninja," the samurai says, drawing his long sword. The other two men slowly move to either side of you.

➦ *To stand your ground and fight, turn to page* **28**.

➦ *To run, turn to page* **30**.

A shuriken's five points could be dipped in deadly poison.

You reach for your own sword, a small katana. But at the last moment, you change your mind and instead grab a shuriken. It is tipped with poison. If you can kill the samurai, you might have a chance. But as you begin to throw it, the other two men are upon you.

Acting purely on instinct, you dart to the left, avoiding a slash of a sword. You strike out with a sweeping kick, knocking one of your attackers off of his feet. You spin to face the other.

With a flick of the wrist, the shuriken hums through the air and sinks into the stomach of your attacker. The blade rips deep into his flesh. The man doubles over and falls to the ground, moaning. You can only hope he stays down, because the samurai is upon you.

29

Turn to page 38.

You're an excellent fighter. But you're no fool. A samurai might think fleeing is dishonorable, but you're no samurai. You turn and sprint away from trouble. Your hope of capturing Kuranosuke has been dashed. You see smoke rising from all around the castle, meaning you've missed out on that part of the mission as well. This is a major victory, but you know that you did little to help.

Turn to page 36.

You nod. "You're right. Doshun might be able to use this information. It's too valuable to risk."

The two of you silently move back to where you entered. You are two dark figures cloaked by shadow. You climb to the top of the wall, and Tozawa begins his descent. As he moves carefully down the wall, you hear shouting behind you. You've been spotted!

"Hurry!" you call to Tozawa.

An arrow whizzes past your head, barely missing you. You grab the rope of your kaginawa. Quickly, you throw yourself over the edge before the enemy can take another shot. In seconds, you and Tozawa are back on solid ground, hurrying back to camp.

Turn the page.

Breathlessly, you tell Doshun what you've learned about the enemy's defenses. He gives you a long, cold look. But the value of your information outweighs any anger he has at you for going on your own.

"Your information will make it much easier to select targets," Doshun says. "We will attack tomorrow night."

With that, Doshun is gone. You smile, knowing that your actions will give Yoshikata's army an advantage in the upcoming battle. You look forward to returning home and telling your family about your adventures.

THE END

To follow another path, turn to page 11.
To read the conclusion, turn to page 101.

Ninja used their skills for both daytime and nighttime missions.

"We'll leave soon," you whisper. "But first, let's let them know we were here."

To reach the storeroom, you have to cross an open courtyard. There are guards on top of the walls, but you guess that they'll be watching outward, not inside toward you. Quickly, you scurry across the open area. You reach the outer wall of the storeroom and duck into the shadows.

Turn the page.

Ninja missions often involved throwing others into a state of confusion.

You take a small measure of gunpowder and spread it along the wooden base of the building. As Tozawa keeps watch, you use a piece of flint rock to strike a spark. The spark hits the gunpowder. Whoosh! Almost instantly, the old wood is on fire. In a few minutes, the storeroom will be a roaring blaze.

"Let's go!" you tell Tozawa.

You follow Tozawa as he darts back across the courtyard. The sound of voices rises behind you. The guards have seen the fire!

"Ninja!" you hear someone shout. That's followed by the sound of an arrow whizzing through the air. Ahead of you, Tozawa falls to the ground, groaning. You keep running, no longer trying to remain unnoticed.

You reach the wall and hurl your kaginawa to the top. You grab the rope and begin climbing as fast as you can. Another arrow bounces off the wall, just missing you.

You're almost to the top! But as you reach for the top of the wall, a sharp pain bites into your back. Your hand goes numb, and you lose your grip. As you plunge to the ground, you realize that the fall will kill you. And that's a good thing. If you lived, the enemy's punishment would likely be far worse than death.

THE END

To follow another path, turn to page 11.
To read the conclusion, turn to page 101.

35

Smoke rises above the castle as the flames spread. Panic has set in among Kuranosuke's people. The castle's defenses are down. Yoshikata wastes no time in launching his attack. His army storms through the castle's front gates, taking advantage of the confusion Doshun and his ninja have created.

Kuranosuke's forces have no chance. They are overwhelmed. Yoshikata's men quickly capture the castle and the enemy. He has Doshun's brilliant plan to thank for his victory. You and your fellow ninja will be paid well.

THE END

To follow another path, turn to page 11.
To read the conclusion, turn to page 101.

There's nothing you can do. The samurai has destroyed your plans. With a sudden burst of speed, you turn and dash away from the gate. You can see Tozawa ahead. Two guards are closing in on him.

Tozawa slams his body into a guard. Tozawa and the guard crash to the ground. You catch up just in time to confront the second guard. With a swift punch, you send him to his knees, his nose bleeding. Tozawa and you run off, knowing that any delay could mean death. It's only a matter of time before archers have you in their sights.

But no arrows come. Quickly, you hurry back to camp. Your mission has failed. But you know you'll get another chance. Doshun will have a plan. You hope his plan is better than yours was.

THE END

To follow another path, turn to page 11.
To read the conclusion, turn to page 101.

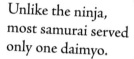

Unlike the ninja, most samurai served only one daimyo.

You manage to draw your katana, but you are at a great disadvantage. The samurai attacks, raining down heavy blows with his sword. A ninja specializes in secrecy and the element of surprise. You realize too late that facing a samurai in single combat was a bad choice.

The samurai continues slashing his sword, showing no weakness. An especially powerful blow sends you to the ground, knocking your katana from your grasp. The weapon clangs away, out of reach. Your last image is of the samurai smiling down at you as he raises his sword for one final strike.

Your only regret is that you won't live to tell your daughter about the siege of the castle.

THE END

To follow another path, turn to page 11.
To read the conclusion, turn to page 101.

Huge armies marched under Japan's warlords during the Age of the Warring States.

CHAPTER 3

Battling Nobunaga

You squint as you look over the horizon. Thick black smoke stings your eyes and clouds your view. You are a ninja of the Iga province. You were born here and have served as a ninja for more than 20 years. But now, everything you know is threatened. Your homeland and your way of life are under attack.

An army of thousands of soldiers marches through Iga, burning everything in its path. The army is approaching the town of Ueno in Iga. You are doing all you can to slow it down.

Turn the page.

Daimyo Oda Nobunaga led the attack against the province of Iga.

Oda Nobunaga commands the enemy army. Nobunaga is the most powerful daimyo in Japan. Two years ago, in 1579, Nobunaga's son, Oda Nobukatsu, tried to conquer Iga. The warriors of Iga turned him away. People say that Nobunaga took this as a personal insult to his family name. This time, he means to finish what his son could not. Some 4,000 Iga warriors, many trained as ninja, face more than 40,000 of Nobunaga's men.

A fellow ninja and friend, Kato, walks up to you. Together, you and Kato lead a small band of fighters. Your job is to scout out the enemy's movements and slow them down whenever you can. The ninja of Iga don't have enough manpower to make a direct stand against Nobunaga's forces. Instead, you have to rely on hit-and-run tactics.

"We could attack them from those woods there," Kato suggests. He points to a well-covered area that the army will soon pass.

"Or we could hit them from within their own ranks," you say. "We have stolen uniforms. We could blend in and do our damage that way."

➤ To take a position in the woods, turn to page **44**.

➤ To disguise yourself as enemy soldiers, turn to page **46**.

You and Kato decide that a quick hit-and-run attack from the woods is the best choice. You and your fighters stay out of sight, well away from the road. You quietly move into the wooded area. The enemy army will be marching past this area shortly. You send several scouts to choose the best spot for an ambush.

Soon, your scouts report back to you. The army will be here in moments. There are two good places from which to attack. "There is a spot that rises over a small creek," explains Naito, a young ninja who is seeing his first real battle. "It has a narrow, open view to the road. Archers could fire several volleys before the enemy soldiers know what hit them."

Another scout suggests a different option. "Where the road narrows, we could hit the enemy in crossfire. We'll use guns and bows to hit the enemy from both sides."

Both samurai and ninja were skilled with bows and arrows.

It is a more dangerous plan, but the narrowed road would allow you to target some of the enemy's leaders.

➤ To set archers on the open rise, turn to page **48**.

➤ To try to trap the enemy in crossfire, turn to page **49**.

You order your fighters to fall back and defend a nearby village while you and Kato dress in stolen enemy uniforms. You wait in the woods until the army begins to pass. Then you simply blend in. Ninja are masters of disguise, and the enemy never suspects a thing.

The sun is quickly setting. The enemy army stops to make camp. This will be your chance.

"What is our target?" Kato asks. "I saw some supply wagons that we could burn."

You scratch your chin as you think. Burning supply wagons would certainly be a good way to weaken the enemy. But you're thinking bigger. Nobunaga himself is with this army. If you could get close enough, maybe you could end the threat to Iga altogether.

You suggest the idea, and Kato gasps. "That's crazy! There is no way we could get close enough. We should hit the supply wagons. That will hurt them. Dying in a failed assassination attempt won't hurt them at all."

➤ *To go after the supply wagons, turn to page 51.*

➤ *To try to assassinate Nobunaga, turn to page 53.*

"Let's move to the open rise," you say. "It's less risky. We can hit them, regroup, and then hit them again."

Your men move to the rise. From far away, it is well covered. A narrow opening to the main road gives you an excellent view. Your group has skilled archers, and they will be ready.

You and Kato scout ahead on foot. You don't have to go far before you spot the marching army. Kato hurries back to tell your men. Meanwhile, you keep your eye on the advancing soldiers. Enemy scouts travel ahead of the group. You notice a pair of them on horseback riding in the direction of the ambush point. If they discover your men, the element of surprise is gone. You can't let that happen.

➤ To try to kill the enemy scouts, turn to page 54.

➤ To warn your men, turn to page 57.

"The best way to hurt the enemy is to kill its leaders," you say. "Let's set up the crossfire."

The ambush point is perfect. Thick brush covers both sides of the road. You station half of your men on each side. Kato goes with one group, while you stay with the other.

You don't have archery skills, so instead you hold a long-barreled gun called a musket. The action will happen quickly, so you will probably get just one shot. With the skill of the ninja, you and your men blend into the brush. Even if the enemy is looking for you, they're not likely to spot you until you begin attacking.

Soon, the army is passing. Soldiers march past by the hundreds. None of them suspect that you're there. Finally, officers on horseback begin filing past. This is it. With a short, sharp whistle, you give the order to attack.

Turn the page.

Arrows whiz through the air. The enemy shouts with surprise. Several officers fall from their horses. You rise up and lift your gun. You spot an officer on horseback and fire. The shot strikes the man in the chest, and he slumps and falls.

The enemy is quickly regrouping. You have to decide whether to attack again or order a retreat. This is a great chance to further hurt the enemy, but staying here will be a huge risk to your men.

➤ *To order a retreat, turn to page **59**.*

➤ *To attack again, turn to page **60**.*

Kato is right. The supply wagons are a target you have a good chance to hit. The two of you move through the camp, keeping your heads down to avoid attention. The soldiers are settling in. The smell of fish and rice cooking over a fire fills the air. It makes you hungry, but you need to finish your mission.

The supply wagons are along the edge of the camp. Several armed soldiers guard them. Your plan is simple. You will set fire to the wagons. You just have to get close to them.

Turn the page.

"We could sneak around the back, alongside those tents," Kato suggests, pointing. "If we each start on a wagon, we can set two fires and double the damage."

"That way, we're in danger of being seen," you point out. "What if you distract the guards while I set a blast?"

"I can do that too," Kato agrees. "It's your decision, but we'll do more damage if we both go."

➤ To have Kato distract the guards, turn to page 63.

➤ To try to sneak in together, turn to page 65.

"We want to hurt the enemy," you say. "What better way than to kill their leader?"

Kato sighs. You can tell he doesn't like the idea, but he goes along with it. Guards move all around the camp's headquarters. Nobunaga surrounds himself with his men. But maybe you can use that against him. You will pose as guards to get close to the daimyo. When you do, you'll kill him. You probably won't escape alive, but saving Iga from Nobunaga will be worth your sacrifice.

The two of you walk confidently toward Nobunaga's tent. Several guards ignore you, but as you near the tent, one guard stops you.

"Who are you?" he asks in an accusing tone. "You don't belong here."

➤ To kill the guard, turn to page 67.

➤ To try to talk your way out of it, turn to page 68.

You can't risk letting the scouts discover your ambush. It's up to you to stop them. The scouts are on horseback, while you are on foot. You can't outrun them. You have to get their attention. You do the only thing you can think of — you scream at them.

The scouts pull up and turn toward you. You make sure they get a good look at you before you turn and run. Sure enough, the scouts run after you. You duck behind a large boulder and draw your katana. Moments later, the scouts gallop past on their horses.

You spring into action, slashing your katana above your head toward the lead rider. The blade glances off his boot, but the sudden attack frightens the horse. It rears back and throws the scout. He lands on the ground with a thud. You quickly drive your katana into his chest.

Ninja often used the element of surprise during their missions.

The other scout digs his heels into his horse, intent on fleeing. But you're ready. You pull a shuriken from your belt and fling it through the air. The blades of the weapon dig into the man's back. He cries out as he slides off his horse and crashes to the ground.

Your quick action has done the job. The enemy army continues to march, knowing nothing of the ambush ahead.

Turn the page.

Minutes after you return to your men, the attack is on. As soon as the marching soldiers are in sight, you order the archers to fire. Arrows hiss through the air. Enemy soldiers scream in pain and shock as the arrows find their targets. Five . . . 10 . . . 20 enemy soldiers fall before you have to retreat.

Turn to page 59.

There are two of them, on horseback, and you're all alone. You don't want to attack with those odds. Instead you rush back to the ambush point, ready to warn your men.

Unfortunately, the scouts are moving faster on horseback than you can run. The scouts don't discover you, but you also don't get a chance to warn your men. Before you reach the ambush point, you meet Kato and the other men. They're running in your direction.

"What happened?" you ask Kato. "Did the enemy scouts attack?"

"Yes, they fired on us," Kato replies, trying to catch his breath. "Luckily, their arrows didn't hit us. The scouts have already turned back to warn the army of the ambush ahead. We have to pull back."

Turn the page.

You reluctantly agree. "It is my fault," you say. "I should have attacked the scouts when I had the chance. Now Nobunaga's men will be able to march through safely."

You've failed in your mission. You will have to hope for another chance to use your skills to defend your home.

THE END

To follow another path, turn to page 11.
To read the conclusion, turn to page 101.

"Retreat!" you shout. The enemy is still confused and disorganized. If you're going to get away, you have to do it now. As one, you and your men spring to your feet and dart back into the brush.

Behind you, you hear gunfire. The enemy has finally organized a response. But you're already well out of range. Your men know the area. They'll easily outrun any chase. You will regroup at a nearby village and plan your next attack.

Your small attack has barely made a dent in Nobunaga's massive army. But these small, quick attacks are the only chance you and your fellow ninja of Iga have. You may have little chance of victory, but Japan will know that Iga did not fall easily.

THE END

To follow another path, turn to page 11.
To read the conclusion, turn to page 101.

"Hit them again!" you yell. You throw the gun over your shoulder, knowing you won't have time to reload it. Instead, you pull a shuriken from your belt. You fling it at the nearest soldier you see.

Meanwhile, the archers are pulling back on their bows to fire. Again, the arrows fly through the air. Some of them find their mark. But the enemy has had time to respond. The sound of gunfire fills the air. You hear the groans of several of your men as they're hit.

"Retreat!" you shout. But as you stand to run, you hear another shot. You double over in pain. You've been hit squarely in the back. Instantly, you know you won't be getting away. Neither will many of your fellow ninja. You got greedy, you realize. You should have retreated when you had a chance.

Oda Nobunaga survived a ninja assassination attempt but was later killed by one of his own men.

You'll die without medical treatment. But if you let yourself be captured, you'll be questioned and forced to give up important secrets. That leaves only one choice. With a battle cry, you draw your katana and charge out among the enemy. The curved blade hums through the air as you cut down one enemy soldier after another. But you're hopelessly outnumbered.

Turn the page.

You feel a knife drive into your back. Then an arrow smashes into your shoulder. The impact throws you to the ground. Your last vision is of dozens of enemy soldiers crowding in on you, each of them eager to deliver the death blow. The defenders of Iga will have to get along without you.

THE END

To follow another path, turn to page 11.
To read the conclusion, turn to page 101.

"Do what you can to distract the guards," you whisper. "I'll set the middle wagon on fire. It might spread to the others before they can stop the blaze."

With a nod, Kato is off. You watch from the shadows as he approaches the guards. You can't hear what he's saying, but the guards don't appear alarmed. It's time to move.

You sneak along a row of small tents, staying in the shadows. Years of practice have taught you to move without making a sound. You soon reach your target. The wagon is old and should catch fire easily. You pull out your tinderbox. Within minutes, you have a small flame flickering. You just hope Kato keeps the guards' attention long enough so they don't notice the orange glow.

Turn the page.

Soon the flames spread to the wood at the base of the wagon. You take some gunpowder from a bamboo tube and place the gunpowder several feet from the flames. Quickly, you move away from the wagon.

"Fire!" someone shouts. Guards rush toward the wagon just as the flame ignites the gunpowder you left. Boom! The explosion echoes through the camp.

In the confusion, you and Kato slip away from the camp. You return to your men, happy that you completed your mission. The attacks will continue tomorrow. They might never be enough, but you know you'll keep defending your home as long as you can.

THE END

To follow another path, turn to page 11.
To read the conclusion, turn to page 101.

Japanese used wagons with two wheels instead of four like in the West.

"You're right," you say. You point at one of the supply wagons. "You take that one. I'll sneak over to the one by the tents. Start your fire and then use the confusion to escape back to the village."

Kato nods and disappears into the darkness. You move carefully, keeping to the shadows. The wagon you plan to burn stands alongside a row of small tents. The tents provide good cover. Nobody is looking in your direction. Everything is going perfectly.

Turn the page.

Suddenly, you hear a shout. Guards rush toward the other wagon. Kato has been spotted!

There's nothing you can do for your friend. He'll have to use his own skills to escape. While the guards are chasing him, you know you have an opening. Quickly, you grab your tinderbox and begin lighting a fire. The wagon is made of old, dry wood and catches fire quickly. Before anyone notices the orange glow, you sneak away.

As you leave, you hear men shouting. They've either captured or killed Kato. You hope for your friend's sake that they didn't take him alive.

You are safe. An enemy supply wagon is in flames. But the price for this is the life of a friend and a respected ninja. Somehow, it doesn't seem worth it.

THE END

To follow another path, turn to page 11.
To read the conclusion, turn to page 101.

66

Quickly, you draw your katana and stab the guard. He falls to the ground, but his screams of pain raise the alarm. Suddenly, dozens of enemy soldiers are bearing down on you.

You and Kato fight back-to-back. You pull a shuriken from your belt and let it fly. The star's blades bury themselves deep into the chest of a guard. Kato uses his katana to kill another.

But there are too many of them. A loud blast fills the air — a gunshot! You hear Kato's moans behind you. He's been shot, and you're next.

You grasp your katana and charge into the enemy. You'll be shot any moment, but at least you can go down fighting. What more could a ninja ask?

THE END

To follow another path, turn to page 11.
To read the conclusion, turn to page 101.

This man knows that you're not guards. "We come with an important message for the daimyo," you explain.

"Give me the message," the guard says warily.

"We need to see the daimyo," you insist.

The man hesitates before calling over two other guards. He turns and whispers something to them. As you watch, you hope they'll let you pass. But then you notice one guard's hands moving toward a weapon at his belt.

Kato notices it too. "Run!" he shouts as he launches himself at the guards. He is sacrificing himself in hopes that you will escape.

You hesitate. Your instinct is to help your friend. But it is hopeless. Joining the fight won't help Kato. You turn and run, dodging some of the guards and crashing into others.

To your shock, you're almost to the edge of the camp. You might get out of here alive. But then, you trip and fall face-first onto the ground. You feel a burning sensation in the middle of your back. It's an arrow. You realize that it has pierced your heart.

You have failed in your mission. At least death will come quickly.

THE END

To follow another path, turn to page 11.
To read the conclusion, turn to page 101.

Tokugawa Ieyasu was a strong daimyo who respected the ninja

CHAPTER 4

The Band of Iga

A bright sun rises over Edo Castle. The castle lies in the city of Edo in southeastern Honshu. You and several other ninja walk alongside Tokugawa Ieyasu, one of the most powerful men in Japan. The stout leader barks out orders as he walks.

Ieyasu is a strong leader who has long been a friend to the ninja. Unlike many daimyo, who distrust the ninja, he has made them his closest allies and personal bodyguards. You are among these men, known as the Band of Iga.

71

Turn the page.

The Band of Iga was once led by the most famous ninja in history, Hattori "Devil" Hanzo. Hanzo served Ieyasu for years before his death in 1590. Like Hanzo, you and your fellow ninja have pledged your lives to protect Ieyasu.

Indeed, Ieyasu's life needs protecting. During his rise to power, he has made powerful enemies. Among them is the daimyo Ishida Mitsunari.

Your spies have warned you that Mitsunari is plotting to kill Ieyasu. Your job is to make sure that this doesn't happen.

Ieyasu is preparing to travel to the nearby village of Soka. His journey will put him in danger of an attack.

Several ninja are going ahead to scout out the route. Others are staying by Ieyasu's side, ready to defend him from any threat.

73

➤ *To join the scouts, turn to page **74**.*

➤ *To stay by Ieyasu's side, turn to page **76**.*

The large city of Edo later became Japan's capital, Tokyo

You and two other ninja, Dai and Sasaki, strike out to check the road ahead. You don't want to attract any attention. You dress as poor commoners and ride old, tired-looking horses. As you ride across the rolling landscape, you scan the area for threats. You cross through wooded areas and across a bridge, but nothing seems out of the ordinary.

You enter the village of Soka on the main road and find a stable for your horses. Many travelers come through here on their way to and from Edo. People fill the streets. Merchants sell food, tools, medicine, and many other items.

"This would be a perfect place for an ambush," whispers Dai. You nod slowly, scanning the scene.

An old man is busy tending his fruit stand. A younger man stands alone near the stand. As your glance sweeps across him, he quickly looks at the ground. He has been watching you.

You split from the other ninja and walk casually toward the fruit stand to get a better look at the man. But as soon as he sees you coming, he turns and darts in the opposite direction.

➧ To chase the man, turn to page 77.

➧ To keep looking for other threats, turn to page 79.

Your place is by Ieyasu's side. Others can go to scout the road ahead. As Ieyasu tends to some business, you prepare for the trip. After all the supplies are loaded, Ieyasu mounts a powerful horse. You position your horse to his right, and another ninja rides to his left. Others travel in front and behind.

You have received no warnings from the ninja ahead, so this part of the road must be safe. But as you enter a wooded area, you sense something is wrong. As a ninja, you are trained to recognize even the smallest clues. The branches of several shrubs are bent back. Footprints lead off the road. Someone has recently walked here. Your instincts are telling you there is danger.

➤ *To stop and investigate, turn to page* **81**.
➤ *To get out of the area quickly, turn to page* **83**.

"Stop!" you shout as you chase the man. He leaps over a fence and darts into a busy street. You expertly clear the fence and follow. You catch a glimpse of him ducking behind a small building.

He thinks he has lost you. Silently, you creep around to the other side of the building. He never sees you coming. Before he knows it, you have a blade to his throat.

"Tell me what you know, and I might spare your life," you whisper.

The man struggles, but you press the blade harder against his skin.

"My partner and I plan to kill Ieyasu," the man admits.

"Where is your partner?" you demand, pressing the blade more firmly against his neck.

Turn the page.

The man's voice cracks as he speaks. "He is at the fruit stand, posing as a merchant."

He's lying. You can hear it in his voice. He isn't going to reveal his partner's true location. He is of no more use to you.

➤ *To kill the man, turn to page* **88**.

➤ *To let him go, turn to page* **90**.

Daimyo hired ninja as scouts to make sure their traveling routes were safe.

You decide chasing the man will take up too much time. You, Dai, and Sasaki carefully search the road and find nothing else suspicious. "The road is clear," you say. "Ieyasu should be safe."

Several hours later, the daimyo and his traveling party arrive. Villagers watch with interest as Ieyasu enters the city sitting high on his horse. His bodyguards ride on each side of him. They are alert and carefully watching everyone, but you can tell they are confident. After all, you haven't reported any threats.

Turn the page.

Suddenly, Ieyasu's horse rears back in terror. The daimyo falls to the ground in a cloud of dust. You see an arrow embedded in the horse's neck. It was intended for Ieyasu!

There! You see a man with a bow, drawing back another arrow. Quickly, you reach for your belt, where you have several shuriken, or throwing stars. But before you can do anything, one of your fellow ninja leaps on the assassin. The ninja's katana runs through the man's stomach. The rest of the ninja gather protectively around Ieyasu.

Turn to page **96**.

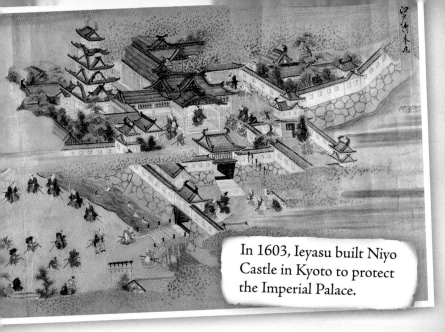

In 1603, Ieyasu built Niyo Castle in Kyoto to protect the Imperial Palace.

You hold up a hand and tell the others to wait. You dismount, kneel, and inspect tracks heading away from the road. You scout the area, searching for any sign of danger.

The snapping of a twig in the distance tells you that someone is nearby. Someone who doesn't want to be seen. You were right — there is danger here. You move to Ieyasu's side.

"Someone is here," you whisper. "We should turn back."

Turn the page.

The daimyo gives you a long look. "I will trust your judgment," he says. "But you must be sure. The day is lost if we turn around now."

You'd hate to be wrong and send Ieyasu back to Edo for no good reason. You could scout further to find out for sure. But that would mean you would have to leave Ieyasu's side. If an attack comes, every ninja will be needed to protect him.

→ To turn back, turn to page 87.

→ To keep scouting, turn to page 92.

"Go!" you shout. Your horses break into a gallop as you race over the road. Suddenly, you spot movement ahead. Assassins!

One assassin aims a long-barreled gun at the road. But your speed surprises him. He fires and misses. You sneer at the man as you speed past. You have no faith in guns. Many people think of them as great new weapons. But you believe they're unreliable. You would rather depend on your katana and your fighting skills.

Soon the danger is behind you. You reach the village of Soka without any more trouble. You ride into a bustling market. Vendors sell fruits, vegetables, meat, tools, and other items.

But strangely, the ninja sent ahead to scout are nowhere to be found. You can't imagine why they would fail to report. Were they killed in an ambush on the road?

Turn the page.

There's no time to wait. You need to get Ieyasu to a safer location. Just then, you spot something out of the corner of your eye. A man dressed as a street vendor has moved closer. He's reaching for a shuriken. He is an assassin!

➤ *To shout a warning to Ieyasu, go to page 85.*

➤ *To throw your body in front of Ieyasu, turn to page 94.*

Ninja used many throwing weapons called shuriken.

"Look out!" you shout. But it's too late.
The assassin, an enemy ninja, is throwing the
shuriken. Its five sharp blades are almost certainly
dipped in deadly poison.

Toda, another ninja bodyguard, reacts more
quickly than you do. Toda grabs Ieyasu, knocking
him from his horse. Together, the two men crash
to the dusty ground. The assassin's shuriken zips
through the air harmlessly.

Turn the page.

The chase is on. Several bodyguards run after the man into the streets. You stay and search the gathering crowd for any further threats. Seeing nothing, you join the chase down the dusty road.

Up ahead, you see the bodyguards tackle the enemy ninja. One of them looks up at you. "Where is Ieyasu?" he asks. "Did you leave him alone with only Toda to guard him?"

You realize that you've neglected your duty to protect Ieyasu. You rush back to find the daimyo brushing the dust off his clothing. He appears otherwise unhurt.

Turn to page 96.

Your instinct tells you there's trouble here. "Go back," you tell the traveling party. The ninja stay close to Ieyasu as you turn and get back on your horse.

"There's someone over there," shouts one of the bodyguards, pointing to some thick brush just off of the road ahead.

"Go! Go!" you shout. You hang back a bit while the rest of the party races back toward Edo. The figure steps out onto the road, carrying a katana. The man — or woman, you can't be sure — is dressed in the dark clothes of a ninja. A cowl covers the ninja's face.

➸ To chase the enemy ninja, turn to page **97**.

➸ To let the enemy ninja go, turn to page **99**.

Daimyo paid ninja for their service after their mission was completed.

Quickly, you thrust the blade into the man's heart. You have been trained to kill quickly, and the man dies almost instantly. You let his body slump to the ground, hoping no one will notice it for at least a few minutes. You don't regret having to kill him. He was the enemy, on a mission to kill Ieyasu.

You gather your fellow ninja. "There are more assassins in the village," you explain. You check the merchant at the fruit stand. He is an old man with no weapons. He is not a part of the plot.

Hours later, Ieyasu's group reaches the village. You tell them what you've learned, and everyone is on the highest alert. But no attack comes. Perhaps you have scared them off. Or maybe the enemy could not pull off their plan without the man you killed. In any case, Ieyasu is safe — for now. You have served him well.

THE END

To follow another path, turn to page 11.
To read the conclusion, turn to page 101.

You know that according to the ninja code, you should kill this man now. But it might draw unwanted attention. He's already given you important information that an assassin is targeting Ieyasu. With a shove, you let the man go. He darts off into the street.

You run to find Dai and Sasaki and tell them what you've learned. "We've got to get back to warn Ieyasu!" you exclaim breathlessly.

"You should have killed the enemy," says Dai with disgust. "We don't leave enemies alive. It's not the ninja way." Sasaki nods.

Smarting from the anger of the other two, you hurry back on the road to Edo. Soon, you meet Ieyasu's traveling party. You tell them that the village is not safe. But you get no thanks for what you've learned. Ieyasu barely looks at you. You had a chance to kill the enemy, but you failed.

You keep your head down as you ride back to Edo Castle with Ieyasu and his party. Once you reach the castle, Ieyasu asks to see you. His face is cold and grim.

"I'm dismissing you from service," he tells you. "You have proven yourself unreliable."

You know there is nothing you can say to defend yourself. In shame, you leave Edo Castle. You successfully protected the daimyo. But by leaving an enemy alive, you shamed yourself as a ninja.

THE END

To follow another path, turn to page 11.
To read the conclusion, turn to page 101.

You nod slowly. "Wait here," you whisper. You signal your fellow ninja to take a close defensive position.

You step off the road into the brush. Years of training have taught you to walk so carefully that you barely make a sound. Staying low to the ground, you creep ahead.

You notice signs that people have passed through this brush recently. Branches are broken and bent. There are tracks in the dirt that don't belong to any animal.

Then you catch a glimpse of a person in the distance. You inch closer to get a good look. The man is carrying a gun! This is surely an assassination attempt.

Your instinct is to kill the man. If you could move just a little closer, you could use a shuriken. But it's more important that you warn Ieyasu. You turn to go back.

A figure stands before you, a long sword in hand. The enemy ninja runs the sword through your stomach before you can even cry out. You slump to the ground, clutching the wound. Blood pours from the wound as your eyes slowly close one last time. You can only hope that Ieyasu gets out alive.

THE END

To follow another path, turn to page 11.
To read the conclusion, turn to page 101.

Ieyasu became shogun, or military leader, of Japan in 1603.

You launch yourself into the air as the assassin throws his weapon. The metal glints in the sunlight as it flies through the air. But you've timed your leap perfectly. The blades dig into the flesh of your shoulder with a burning pain. You crash to the ground.

The other ninja swarm over the attacker. Ieyasu ducks low to the ground by your side.

"Thank you," Ieyasu says, breathless. He looks at the blood dripping from your shoulder. "It does not look serious. I think you will be all right."

But you know better. The enemy would have dipped the blades into a deadly poison. Already, you feel its effect on your body.

You lie there on the ground, looking up at one of the most powerful men in Japan. The bright light of the sun dims as your vision fades. The daimyo is safe, but his safety has cost you your life.

THE END

To follow another path, turn to page 11.
To read the conclusion, turn to page 101.

The assassination plot has failed. Ieyasu is alive and well. But with shame, you realize that you were of little help.

Ieyasu stands before you. The disappointment in his face is clear. He doesn't say a word to you, but he doesn't have to. You already know. When you return to Edo, you'll be released from his service. Your days with the Band of Iga are over.

THE END

To follow another path, turn to page 11.
To read the conclusion, turn to page 101.

You pull on the reins of your horse and spin around. The two of you are alone. This ninja is a threat. If you allow the ninja to live, he or she is almost sure to make an attempt on Ieyasu's life. You can't let that happen. With your katana in hand, you charge at the ninja.

You swing the curved sword as you race past, but the ninja sidesteps the attack. The enemy flings a shuriken, which strikes your horse in the rear. It is not enough to seriously hurt your horse, but the animal charges forward in pain. You fall from the horse's back and land on the ground.

The impact dazes you for a moment. As your mind clears, you realize you dropped your katana. The enemy stands above you, sword in hand.

Turn the page.

You know that your end is near. The ninja will finish you off at any moment. But to your surprise, the ninja only bows slightly, and then disappears into the trees.

Your enemy has spared your life. It's not the ninja way to leave an enemy alive, but you're grateful. You get back on your horse and begin the journey back to Edo. You wonder if you would have made the same choice if the roles were reversed.

THE END

To follow another path, turn to page 11.
To read the conclusion, turn to page 101.

The ninja stares at you. Finally, the ninja bows — just a small tilt of the head. It is a show of respect. Hesitantly, you nod back. This is a fellow ninja, even if he or she is an enemy. No matter what happens, you are members of a brotherhood.

With one last look, you turn and your horse breaks into a gallop, back to Edo. You have a feeling you will cross paths with this ninja again in the future. In a strange way, you find yourself almost looking forward to it.

THE END

To follow another path, turn to page 11.
To read the conclusion, turn to page 101.

Toyotomi Hideyoshi was Nobunaga's successor and helped unify Japan.

CHAPTER 5

The Ninja's Place in History

Medieval Japan was a violent place, full of war and political struggles. The ninja weren't always the most respected members of Japanese society. But they filled an important role to the leaders they served. As great fighters and spies, they were probably the most feared warriors in the land.

101

But the ninja made many enemies along the way. Among them was Oda Nobunaga. In 1581, this powerful daimyo attacked the province of Iga, where many ninja lived. The attack scattered the ninja, and their power began to decrease.

Commodore Matthew Perry (second from left) visited Japan in 1853.

That decline continued in 1603 when Tokugawa Ieyasu reunited Japan. He formed a dynasty that would come to be known as the Tokugawa Shogunate. This dynasty ruled Japan for the next 265 years. With Japan united, the need for secret warriors such as the ninja faded. Fewer young people learned the art of ninjutsu, and soon the ninja were nearly a thing of the past.

The last battle that ninja were reported to have taken part in came in 1638. A small group of ninja helped put down a revolt in a conflict known as the Shimabara Rebellion.

The ninja continued to exist in a limited form for years after that, though. In 1853, American Commodore Matthew Perry sailed to Japan to set up a trading agreement with the Japanese. A ninja disguised as a government official sneaked onto one of Perry's ships to gather information. It is the last known account of ninja activity.

Ninja are popular characters in comic books, TV shows, and movies.

Some people insist that the ninja never disappeared completely. They claim that the traditions were passed down to the modern day. They say ninja masters still exist in the modern world.

Information on how the ninja lived and worked is often incomplete. They were called shadow warriors for a reason, after all. But our imaginations can fill in many of the details. Maybe that's what makes ninja still so fascinating to many people.

Time Line

AD 907 — The Tang Dynasty in China ends, causing many Chinese refugees to flee into Japan. Many of these refugees settle in the Iga and Koga provinces.

940 — Some of the earliest reports of ninjalike activity appear in Japanese history.

1100s — The ninjutsu arts form as a culture. The movement remains very secretive and little is known of the early ninja.

1467 — The Onin War begins the Age of the Warring States, in which ninja play a large role.

1477 — The Onin War ends.

1541 — Hattori "Devil" Hanzo, history's most famous ninja, is born.

1558 — Ninja in the service of Rokkaku Yoshikata use fake enemy lanterns to enter Sawayama Castle and set fire to the castle. Yoshikata's men then capture the castle.

1581 — The daimyo Oda Nobunaga invades Iga, forcing the ninja there to scatter into other provinces. The daimyo Tokugawa Ieyasu takes many of the refugee ninja into his service.

1590 — Hattori Hanzo dies. With Hanzo's ninja at his side, Tokugawa Ieyasu marches into Edo and gains more power.

1603 — Tokugawa Ieyasu becomes shogun and begins the process of reuniting Japan. The Age of the Warring States ends.

1615 — Ninja loyal to the shogun take part in a successful attack on Osaka Castle.

1638 — Ninja help put down a revolt of Christian peasants in the Shimabara Rebellion. It is the last major battle in which ninja are reported to have taken part.

1853 — The final known ninja mission involves a single ninja sneaking on an American ship that is attempting to open Japanese ports to trade.

OTHER PATHS TO EXPLORE

In this book, you've explored a few different roles of the ninja. You've seen that some ninja were loyal servants, while others were mercenaries willing to work and even kill for the highest bidder.

Perspectives on history are as varied as the people who lived it. You can explore other paths on your own to learn more about what happened. Seeing history from many points of view is an important part of understanding it.

Here are some ideas of other ninja points of view to explore:

+ Ninja were used as assassins. What would life be like as a hired killer?

+ Some ninja opened special training schools. What would life have been like as a student of ninjutsu?

+ Some legends tell that ninja were sent as far as the New World to perform missions. What might a ninja mission in colonial America have been like?

READ MORE

Glaser, Jason, and Don Roley. *Ninja*. Mankato, Minn.: Capstone Press, 2006.

Hanel, Rachael. *Samurai*. Mankato, Minn.: Creative Education, 2008.

Ollhoff, Jim. *Ninja*. Edina, Minn.: Abdo, 2008.

Turnbull, Stephen R. *Real Ninja: Over 20 True Stories of Japan's Secret Assassins*. New York: Enchanted Lion Books, 2008.

INTERNET SITES

FactHound offers a safe, fun way to find Internet sites related to this book. All of the sites on FactHound have been researched by our staff.

Here's all you do:

Visit *www.facthound.com*

FactHound will fetch the best sites for you!

GLOSSARY

assassinate (uh-SASS-uh-nate) — to kill someone who is well known or important

daimyo (DIME-yoh) — a powerful landowner in medieval Japanese society

dynasty (DYE-nuh-stee) — a series of rulers belonging to the same family or group

kaginawa (kaw-gee-NAH-wah) — a climbing tool used by ninja

medieval (mee-DEE-vuhl) — concerning the period of history between AD 500 and 1450

mercenary (MUR-suh-nayr-ee) — a soldier who is paid to fight for a foreign army

ninjutsu (nihn-JUH-tsoo) —the martial arts practiced by ninja

province (PROV-uhnss) — a district or a region of some countries

refugee (ref-yuh-JEE) — a person forced to flee his or her home because of natural disaster or war

samurai (SAH-muh-rye) — a skilled Japanese warrior, usually of high social class

shogun (SHOH-gun) — a military leader of Japan

BIBLIOGRAPHY

Deal, William E. *Handbook to Life in Medieval and Early Modern Japan.* New York : Oxford University Press, 2007.

Jansen, Marius B., ed. *Warrior Rule in Japan.* New York: Cambridge University Press, 1995.

Levy, Joel. *Ninja: The Shadow Warrior.* New York: Metro Books, 2007.

Time-Life Books. *What Life Was Like Among Samurai and Shoguns: Japan, AD 1000-1700.* Alexandria, Va.: Time-Life Books, 1999.

Turnbull, Stephen R. *Warriors of Medieval Japan.* New York: Osprey, 2005.

INDEX